# Project Name

# Project Description

# Project Goals

# Project Phases

# Project
# Timeframe

## In details

# Project Costs

## In details

# Project tools and skills

tools and skills that i have for the project

tools and skills that i don't have for the project

# Project Execution

How do i get tools and skills that i don't have

# Divide the project into small tasks

In order

# Evaluations

# Notes